WORLD WAR II

THE VICTORY AND LEGACY OF WORLD WAR II

BY HEATHER C. HUDAK

CONTENT CONSULTANT
Mikkel Dack
Assistant Professor, History
Rowan University

Cover image: Millions of women entered the workforce during World War II. They helped the Allies win the war.

Core Library

An Imprint of Abdo Publishing
abdobooks.com

abdobooks.com

Published by Abdo Publishing, a division of ABDO, PO Box 398166, Minneapolis, Minnesota 55439.

Printed in the United States of America, North Mankato, Minnesota.
052024
092024

Cover Photo: Bettmann/Getty Images
Interior Photos: Corbis Historical/Getty Images, 4–5; Charles Hoff/New York Daily News Archive/Getty Images, 6; Mondadori Portfolio/Getty Images, 10–11; Red Line Editorial, 13, 33; Hulton-Deutsch Collection/Corbis Historical/Getty Images, 16; Bettmann/Getty Images, 18–19, 29; Hum Historical/Alamy, 20; US Army Signal Corps/Interim Archives/Archive Photos/Getty Images, 24, 43; Hulton Archive/Getty Images, 26–27; Shutterstock Images, 36–37; Pandora Pictures/Shutterstock Images, 38, 45

Editor: Marley Richmond
Series Designer: Ryan Gale

Library of Congress Control Number: 2023949126

Publisher's Cataloging-in-Publication Data

Names: Hudak, Heather C., author.
Title: The victory and legacy of world war II / by Heather C. Hudak
Description: Minneapolis, Minnesota: Abdo Publishing, 2025 | Series: World war II | Includes online resources and index.
Identifiers: ISBN 9781098293666 (lib. bdg.) | ISBN 9798384912934 (ebook)
Subjects: LCSH: World War, 1939-1945--Juvenile literature. | Reconstruction (1939-1951)--Juvenile literature. | Peace--Juvenile literature. | War crime trials--Juvenile literature. | Influence (Literary, artistic, etc.)--Juvenile literature. | Politics and government--Juvenile literature.
Classification: DDC 940.53--dc23

CONTENTS

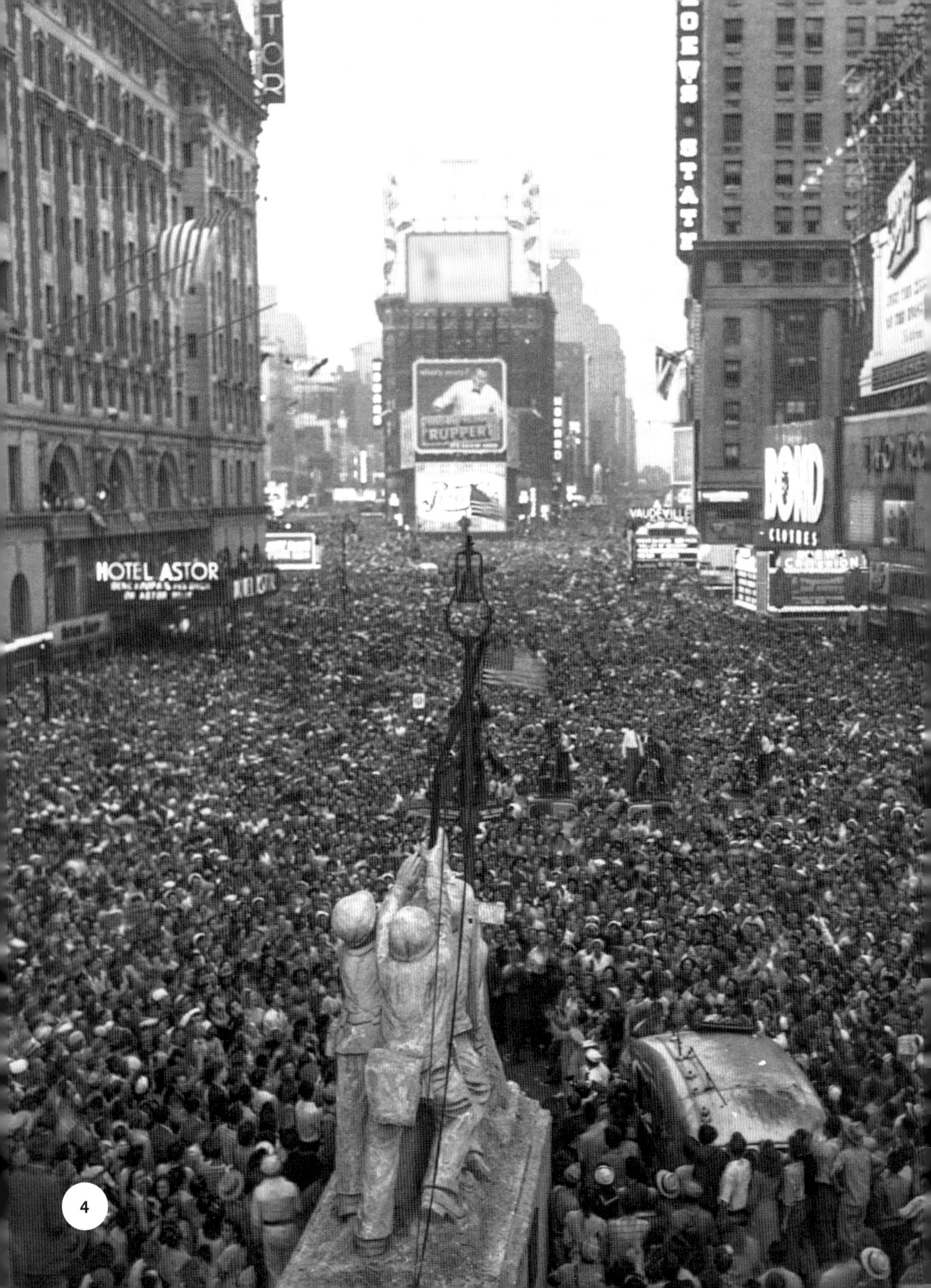
HOTEL ASTOR
RUPPERT
VAUDEVILLE
BOND
CLOTHES

CHAPTER ONE

NEW YORK RISES UP

Hundreds of thousands of people gathered in New York City's Times Square on August 14, 1945. They waited for an announcement from the president declaring an end to World War II (1939–1945). The fighting had ended in Europe months earlier, but it was still raging in the Pacific. Japan was expected to officially surrender that day. Finally, at 7:03 p.m., the crowd got the news it was waiting for.

After years of being shut off during the war, the 15,000 lights of the neon sign on

The crowd in Times Square had grown to more than 2 million people by 10:00 p.m. on August 14, 1945.

When Japan surrendered, the crowd in Times Square cheered, waved flags, and blew horns.

top of the Times Tower flashed to life. They spelled out five words that forever changed the world: "Official—Truman announces Japanese surrender." At that moment, cheering was the only sound for miles around. World War II had finally come to an end.

Japan's surrender signaled the end of the deadliest war in history, a war that had gone on for six years. People all over the world had felt its impact, and now the war was over. The day was one to remember.

JAPANESE SURRENDER

World War II was fought between the Allied powers and the Axis powers. The Allied powers included the

United States, Great Britain, and the Soviet Union. By the end of the war, more than 45 countries had joined the alliance. The eight Axis powers included Germany, Italy, and Japan. The Allied powers fought back against the extreme governments leading the Axis nations and against those governments' attempts to expand their territories.

NEW YORK CITY GOES DARK

In 1928 a neon sign was installed on top of the Times Tower. This building was the home of the *New York Times* newspaper. Each day, the daily news was broadcast on the sign. Times Tower became a symbol of Manhattan. In 1942 the lights of the Times Tower and other New York buildings were turned off. People feared the glittering lights would make it too easy for enemies to bomb the city. The powering down of the Times Tower represented the worst of times for New Yorkers.

Some battles were fought in the European theater, and others were fought in the Pacific. The war in Europe had begun in 1939. Japanese and US forces had been

PERSPECTIVES

HIROHITO TAKES A STAND

Emperor Hirohito played a largely ceremonial role in Japan. Many historians believe he had little power to make decisions for the country, and he often had to comply with military leaders' decisions. By August 1945, Japan's leaders began to debate surrender. Hirohito could not stand to see his country suffer any more than it already had. He feared that the Soviet Union or the United States would invade mainland Japan. Though he did not have a direct role in commanding the military during the war, Hirohito eventually sided with those who wanted peace. He ordered the Japanese government to surrender.

locked in a bloody conflict in the Pacific theater since 1941. By mid-1945 the war in Europe had come to an end. Meanwhile, Japan was running out of resources, and US soldiers were gaining ground. Then the United States dropped two atomic bombs on Japan, causing unimaginable death and destruction.

Finally, on August 15, Japanese emperor Hirohito broadcasted the news of Japan's surrender in a radio announcement. There is a 13-hour time difference between Japan and New York, so the news of Japan's surrender broke in the United States on August 14.

World War II officially came to an end on September 2, 1945. On that day, Japan and the United States signed the paperwork that formalized their agreement. As news of the day's events spread across the globe, people rejoiced.

FURTHER EVIDENCE

Chapter One introduces Japan's surrender at the end of World War II. Identify one of the chapter's main points. What evidence does the author provide to support this point? Watch the video at the website below. Does the information on the website support the main point of the chapter? Does it present new evidence?

JAPANESE SURRENDER

abdocorelibrary.com/victory-legacy-world-war-ii

CHAPTER TWO

VICTORY IN EUROPE

June 6, 1944, was a turning point for World War II in Europe. On that day, Allied forces landed in Normandy, France. France was occupied by Nazi Germany. The Nazi Party, led by Adolf Hitler, was anti-Semitic, extreme, and nationalist. Over the next few months, Allied forces fought their way across the country. By August 1944, they had liberated France from Nazi control. Allied forces then began to work their way toward Germany.

Nearly 133,000 Allied troops landed in Normandy on June 6, 1944. About 7,000 ships participated in the attack that day.

LIBERATION OF NAZI CAMPS

Throughout the 1930s and 1940s, the Nazis had set up camps where they held people prisoner without trials. Jews, communists, and enemies of the state were held in these concentration camps. Prisoners were forced to perform hard labor or be tortured. Many died of disease or starvation.

The Nazis also set up extermination camps where they murdered Jews. Millions of Jews were killed at Nazi camps. It was a mass genocide called the Holocaust. Several other groups were also targeted and killed during this time, including the Roma people.

As Allied forces moved across Europe, they began to liberate concentration camps. The Majdanek camp in Poland was the first major concentration camp to be freed after Soviet soldiers arrived at the site in July 1944. Over the next several months, Allied soldiers freed thousands of prisoners in camps across Europe. But many people died soon after liberation. Few survivors remained.

CONCENTRATION CAMPS FREED

This map shows some of the major Nazi camps, their dates of liberation, and which countries freed them. What does this map show about the reach of Nazi Germany? How does it help you understand the progress of Allied forces as the war in Europe came to an end?

PERSPECTIVES

HOLOCAUST SURVIVORS

Many survivors of concentration camps felt mixed emotions after they were freed. They were excited to leave the camps. However, they felt guilty that they lived when many of their friends and family died. They did not know what to expect as they returned to life outside the camps. Slovakian Holocaust survivor Eva Braun said, "We had survived, and we had to return to civilization, but how did one behave in a normal world? . . . We had nothing. We were frightened that we might not have anyone left in the world."

BATTLE OF BERLIN

By 1945 much of Europe lay in ruins. The United States and Great Britain had relentlessly bombed German cities, including Dresden and Hamburg. Millions of people had died. Great Britain, the United States, and other Western Allied forces were closing in. The Soviet Union's Red Army had contributed greatly to the Allies' progress in Europe, and Soviet forces were also gaining ground in Germany from the east.

On April 16, 1945, Soviet forces began closing in on Berlin, the nation's capital. It was the beginning of the Battle of Berlin, the last major European battle of World War II. The German forces were weak. They could not hold off the Soviets.

Adolf Hitler had retreated into a bunker to protect himself. Finally, by April 25, the Soviets had surrounded Berlin. The city was pounded into rubble. Hitler took his own life on April 30. He did not want to be taken by the enemy. Days later, Berlin fell to the Soviets.

GERMAN SURRENDER

The Allies demanded that Germany unconditionally surrender. Germany was in no position to decline. On May 7, a German general signed the official surrender document in Reims, France. The document stated that the Germans would stop fighting on May 8.

The next day, the Soviets demanded that Germany also surrender separately in the east. On May 8, a second surrender document was signed in Berlin by

US military general Walter Bedell Smith, *center*, signed the documents of surrender for the Allies on May 7, 1945.

a German field marshal and the commander-in-chief of the Soviet Army. The war came to an end in Eastern Europe on May 9. But battles continued to rage in the Pacific.

POTSDAM CONFERENCE

In July 1945, leaders of the Allied powers met in Potsdam, Germany, to discuss the terms of the end of the war. One of the things they discussed was how they would govern Germany. The Allies now had power over the country.

They decided to divide the country into four occupied zones. Each zone was governed by a different nation: the Soviet Union in the northeast, Great Britain in the northwest, France in the southwest, and the United States in the southeast. Berlin, the capital, was in Soviet territory. However, it was split up and governed by all four countries as well.

CELEBRATIONS OF VICTORY

When the war in Europe officially ended, people flocked to the streets in Allied cities. Celebrations took place all over the world. Since 1945 the surrender of Germany has been celebrated on two different dates. Victory in Europe Day takes place in Western Europe on May 8. Meanwhile, the Russians celebrate Victory Day on May 9.

CHAPTER THREE

VICTORY IN THE PACIFIC

When Germany surrendered in Europe, many Allied forces were redeployed to the Pacific, where the war was still going strong. Many Pacific islands were caught in the crossfire of the Allied powers and Japanese forces. The Allies pushed the war closer to mainland Japan.

THE BATTLES OF IWO JIMA AND OKINAWA

In March 1945, US marines captured a small Japanese island called Iwo Jima. The island is

Some US troops returned to the United States after Germany surrendered.

US soldiers and marines cheered as the Battle of Okinawa came to an end.

located 660 miles (1,062 km) from Tokyo, the capital of Japan. Capturing the island was a turning point in the war because it gave the Allied powers a strategic advantage. They could launch planes from the island to bomb mainland Japan. That month, the United States launched a bombing campaign against Tokyo, killing about 100,000 people.

On April 1, more than 60,000 US soldiers and marines landed on the Japanese island Okinawa. The Battle of Okinawa was the last and biggest major battle of World War II, and the United States won. More than

240,000 people died over the course of the battle. The United States showed that it would relentlessly attack Japan until the country surrendered.

JAPANESE DOWNFALL

The battles of Iwo Jima and Okinawa took their toll on Japan. Japan was running out of military resources. The Soviet Union was also preparing to fight in the Pacific.

At the Potsdam Conference, the Allies called on Japan to surrender. Japan rejected the call. Japanese leaders believed the United States did not have the resources to keep up a fight across the Pacific.

NUCLEAR ATTACK

For years top scientists in Germany and the United States had been working to create nuclear weapons. In July 1945, the United States successfully tested the first atomic bomb. It was more powerful than anything the world had seen before. When Japan refused to surrender at the Potsdam Conference, US president

Harry S. Truman and his advisors decided to unleash the new weapon. They wanted to end the war as quickly as possible.

On August 6, the United States dropped an atomic bomb on Hiroshima, Japan. An estimated 80,000 people were killed within minutes. Three days later, the United States dropped a second atomic bomb on Nagasaki, Japan. Within one minute of the explosion, approximately

PATHS TO SURRENDER

By April 1945, US military planners were not sure if Japan would ever surrender. They had begun planning an invasion of mainland Japan called Operation Downfall. Hundreds of thousands of US troops were expected to die in the invasion, alongside 5 to 10 million Japanese people. Military leaders also considered creating a blockade, which would cut off food supplies to Japan. This blockade would kill millions of civilians. In the end, President Truman turned to the atomic bomb instead. Some historians believe that either Operation Downfall or the blockade would have been more deadly than the atomic bombs. Experts still debate this decision.

40,000 people died, and about 25,000 others were injured. Japan could no longer keep up the fight.

JAPAN SURRENDERS

On August 10, the Japanese government agreed to accept the terms of surrender outlined at the Potsdam Conference. However, Japan had one condition: the position of the emperor would remain in place. On August 12, the Allies agreed to accept Japan's condition with the understanding that the emperor would

PERSPECTIVES

JEWEL VOICE BROADCAST

On August 15, 1945, a message from Emperor Hirohito was broadcast over the radio in Japan. This was called the Jewel Voice Broadcast. In his message, Hirohito never spoke about surrender specifically. Instead, he declared the government had a new mission "to strive for the common prosperity and happiness of all nations as well as the security and well-being of our subjects." He said it was in the people's best interest to stop fighting. He said atomic weapons would continue to cause death and destruction if Japan kept up the fight.

US sailors watched military and political leaders sign the Japanese Instrument of Surrender on September 2, 1945.

not have the authority to make decisions for Japan on his own. Finally, on August 14, Japan surrendered. The formal surrender took place on September 2, 1945, aboard the USS *Missouri*. The document of surrender was signed by representatives of the Japanese emperor and government, as well as by representatives of the Allied powers.

From 1945 to 1952, the Allies, led by the United States, occupied Japan. They made big changes. One of the biggest changes was the creation of a new constitution that made Japan more democratic. Japan was not allowed to have a military, and its constitution banned the country from ever going to war again.

STRAIGHT TO THE SOURCE

President Harry S. Truman released an official statement on August 14, 1945. He spoke about Japan's surrender. He said:

> *I have received this afternoon a message from the Japanese government . . . in reply to the message forwarded to that government by the Secretary of State on August 11. I deem this reply a full acceptance of the Potsdam Declaration, which specifies the unconditional surrender of Japan. In the reply there is no qualification.*
>
> *Arrangements are now being made for the signing of the surrender terms at the earliest possible moment.*
>
> Source: "The President's News Conference." *American Presidency Project*, n.d., presidency.ucsb.edu. Accessed 19 Oct. 2023.

CONSIDER YOUR AUDIENCE

Adapt this passage for a different audience, such as a friend or family member. Write a speech conveying this same information to the new audience. How does your post differ from the original text and why?

CHAPTER FOUR

GLOBAL AFTERMATH

During World War II, millions of people lost their lives, including civilians and members of the military. Some estimates say 60 million people died during the war. Other experts say 70 to 85 million. This was more than 3 percent of the world's population at the time. The Soviet Union alone lost more than 25 million people.

Much of Europe, Asia, and parts of Africa were in ruins. Up to 65 million Europeans had been displaced during the war. There were more than 11 million European refugees after

Many troops were buried in cemeteries where they died. Thousands of US marines were temporarily buried in Iwo Jima.

PERSPECTIVES

RADIATION POISONING

When Japanese people first started experiencing radiation poisoning, much of the public did not know why. The United States denied claims that Japanese people's suffering was because of radiation. Leslie Groves was the military official who led the United States' efforts to build the atomic bomb. He did not believe radiation was killing people. He said that radiation poisoning would be a "very pleasant way to die." But Japanese people were indeed suffering from radiation. Its effects were painful and often deadly.

the war ended. Most refugees willingly returned home by September 1945. Others were forced to move to new countries or live in temporary camps.

In Japan, the use of atomic bombs had long-term consequences. Radiation is harmful energy released by nuclear weapons. Many people in Hiroshima and Nagasaki died from radiation poisoning. A number of survivors developed diseases such as cancer.

Some of the highest-ranking Nazi leaders sat in the courtroom as defendants during the Nuremberg trials.

WAR TRIALS

After the war, the Allies put high-ranking leaders from Nazi Germany on trial for war crimes. The trials started in November 1945 and took place in Nuremberg, Germany. In total, 199 people were tried and 161 were convicted. Thirty-seven received the death penalty.

In May 1946, Japanese political and military leaders were tried for the crimes they committed during

World War II. The trials took place in Tokyo. In total, 25 leaders were tried. Seven received the death penalty, and 16 were sentenced to life in prison.

US SUPERPOWER

During World War II, the continental United States was far from the fighting. It did not suffer the same damage as European countries. Instead, the United States had been able to focus on building up industries and increasing production at home.

KEEPING THE PEACE

The United Nations (UN) was established in 1945 to help maintain peace and security. The UN was developed with the support of all Allied powers. The United States, Great Britain, and the Soviet Union designed how the organization would work. The UN was signed into effect on October 24, 1945, with 51 member states. Nearly 200 countries are now members of the UN.

The US economy nearly doubled between 1939 and 1945. By contrast, in Western Europe, the economy decreased by about 18 percent, and

Japan's economy decreased by 50 percent. After the war, the United States had emerged as the world's most important economic and military power.

COLD WAR

The Soviet Union had also emerged from the war as a superpower. The Soviet Union was a Communist country, and it wanted to expand into other parts of Europe. The United States and many democratic nations in Western Europe were against communism.

In 1947 the US government declared it would support countries at risk of falling to communism. The United States also worked to secure its own influence in North and South America. This was the start of the Cold War (1947–1991). During this time, the United States and the Soviet Union became bitter rivals. The two countries also worked to produce bigger, more powerful weapons.

The Soviet Union successfully tested its first nuclear weapon in 1949. Tensions remained high between the

United States and the Soviet Union, but there was no direct violence. Each country knew it could not use nuclear weapons without putting itself at risk.

Soon other countries began developing nuclear weapons as well. Some countries still keep nuclear weapons today. Leaders may believe that these weapons deter other countries from attacking.

GERMANY DIVIDED

In 1948 Great Britain, France, and the United States began to unify their occupation zones in Germany. The Soviet Union did not join them. Soviet leaders feared Germany would become a threat if it was reunified.

Other Western European countries were also concerned. To calm their fears, Great Britain proposed a security alliance in which member countries would come to each other's aid in the event of a threat. The North Atlantic Treaty Organization, commonly known as NATO, was signed into effect on April 4, 1949.

GERMANY
AFTER WORLD WAR II

This map shows how Germany was divided between the major Allied powers after World War II. It also shows how the Allied powers united their zones to create West Germany and the Soviet Union's zone became East Germany. How does this map help you understand what happened to Germany after World War II?

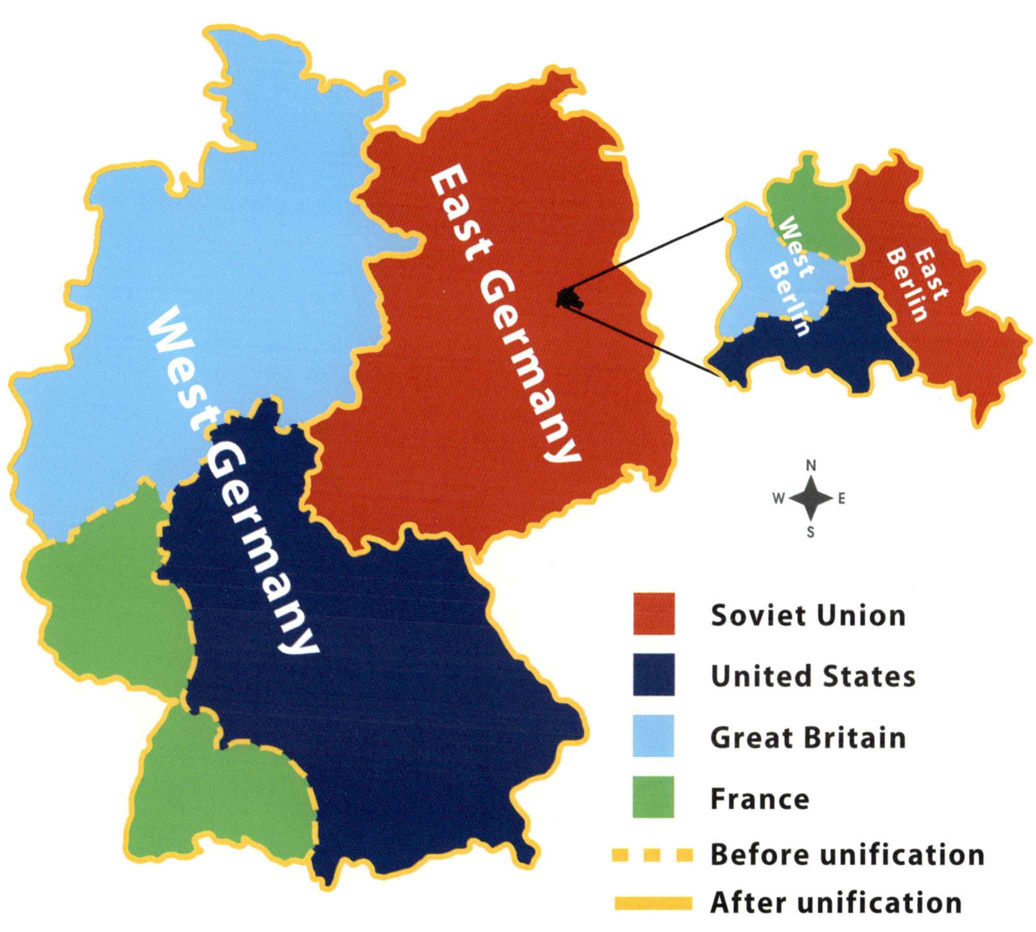

In May 1945, the Western Allies completed the unification of their occupied lands. This became West Germany. In October, the Soviets established East Germany.

BERLIN WALL

People who lived in West Germany had more freedoms than those living in East Germany. The economy was also stronger in West Germany. Many East Germans tried to escape through West Berlin. In August 1961, East German leaders put up a barrier between East Berlin and West Berlin to keep people from fleeing. Over time, it was built into a heavily guarded wall that surrounded West Berlin and ran along the border between East and West Germany.

In the late 1980s, there was pressure on East Germany to give citizens more freedoms. By 1990, the Berlin Wall had been demolished, and East Germany and West Germany were reunified. In 1991, the Soviet Union collapsed. The Cold War had come to an end.

STRAIGHT TO THE SOURCE

In 1963, President John F. Kennedy visited West Berlin. He spoke about the differences between East and West Berlin, and how they showed the danger of communism. Kennedy said:

> *There are many people in the world who really don't understand . . . what is the great issue between the free world and the Communist world. Let them come to Berlin. There are some who say that communism is the wave of the future. Let them come to Berlin. And there are some who say in Europe and elsewhere we can work with the Communists. Let them come to Berlin. . . .*
>
> *Freedom has many difficulties and democracy is not perfect, but we have never had to put a wall up to keep our people in, to prevent them from leaving us.*

Source: "Remarks of John F. Kennedy at the Rudolph Wilde Platz, Berlin, June 16, 1963." *John F. Kennedy Presidential Library and Museum*, n.d., jfklibrary.org. Accessed 7 Nov. 2023.

WHAT'S THE BIG IDEA?

Read the quote from John F. Kennedy carefully. What is the main idea? What details does Kennedy provide to support the main idea? Identify two or three main points.

LEGACY TODAY

World War II ended decades ago, but the legacy of the biggest and deadliest war in history continues today. There are monuments and memorials all over the world dedicated to remembering those who fought and died in the war. These monuments both remind people of the tragic events that occurred between 1939 and 1945 and aim to help prevent anything like World War II from ever happening again.

The Hiroshima Peace Memorial in Hiroshima, Japan, is a reminder of the cost of war. It also remembers the atomic bombing victims.

Gold stars hang on the Freedom Wall at the World War II Memorial. There is one star for every 100 US soldiers who died in the war.

REMEMBERING THE WAR

The World War II Memorial in Washington, DC, opened in 2004. It is dedicated to the Americans who served in the war, as well as those who supported the war effort at home. The memorial features 4,048 gold stars. It also has a sign that reads, "Here we mark the price of freedom."

In 2005, the Women of World War II memorial opened in London, United Kingdom. The bronze statue honors the 7 million women who served in the armed forces during World War II or supported the war effort. These women did not fight in combat, but their roles were essential to the Allied victory.

The Hiroshima Peace Memorial is located at the Genbaku Dome. It was the only building to remain standing in the area where the first atomic bomb exploded. It is a reminder of one of the most destructive days in world history and a symbol of hope for a better future.

The Memorial to the Murdered Jews of Europe

RESEARCH AND DEVELOPMENT

During World War II, US scientists developed and perfected new technologies in support of the war effort. Many inventions continue to benefit people today. One example is the production of penicillin. This medicine fights infections. When soldiers were injured during battle, infections could kill them. But penicillin stops infections that could be deadly. The United States increased production of this medicine during World War II. Penicillin has saved millions of lives since then.

PERSPECTIVES

INCREASE IN ANTI-SEMITISM

Anti-Semitism predates World War II, and it did not end when the war was over. According to the Anti-Defamation League (ADL), an antihate organization, the number of anti-Semitic incidents in the United States continues to grow. The ADL says that people need to learn about anti-Semitism and speak out against it. Many Holocaust survivors agree, including Hershel Greenblatt. He said, "We need . . . meaningful education that teaches against hate."

opened in Berlin in 2005. It is made up of 2,711 concrete slabs covering about 205,000 square feet (19,000 sq m). It is a place for thoughtful reflection and discussions about the Holocaust.

HOLOCAUST SURVIVORS

In 1933, there were about 9.5 million Jews across Europe. That was about 60 percent of the world's Jewish population. By 1950, that number had decreased to 3.5 million. The Nazis and their collaborators killed an estimated 6 million Jewish people during the Holocaust.

Many Jewish survivors moved after the war. Only about one-third of the global Jewish population remained in Europe. Today there are about 16 million Jews worldwide.

People continue to celebrate the end of World War II more than eight decades later. By remembering the past, they hope to prevent similar events in the future. The lasting legacy of World War II can be seen in the memorials, peace-keeping organizations, and international alliances that exist today.

EXPLORE ONLINE

Chapter Five focuses on war memorials and the Holocaust. The website below provides more information about the Holocaust, including its impact and aftermath. Why is it important to remember the war and the Holocaust? What can people learn from this time in history? How can they apply what they learn to their lives today?

INTRODUCTION TO THE HOLOCAUST

abdocorelibrary.com/victory-legacy-world-war-ii

IMPORTANT DATES

July 1944

The Soviets free the Majdanek Nazi camp in Poland. This is the first major concentration camp to be freed.

May 1945

Germany signs documents of surrender on May 7 and 8, ending World War II in Europe.

July 1945

Allied leaders meet in Potsdam, Germany, to discuss the terms of the end of the war.

August 1945

The United States drops the first atomic bomb on Hiroshima, Japan, on August 6. US forces drop a second atomic bomb on Nagasaki, Japan, on August 9.

September 2, 1945

Japan signs the document of surrender. World War II officially comes to an end.

November 1945

The Nuremberg trials begin, and Nazi officials are tried for war crimes.

May 1946

The Tokyo war crimes trials begin.

1947

The Cold War begins between the Soviet Union and the United States.

1990

East and West Germany are reunified.

2005

The Memorial to the Murdered Jews of Europe opens in Berlin.

STOP AND THINK

Take a Stand

The United States dropped atomic bombs on the Japanese cities of Hiroshima and Nagasaki. It was one of the deadliest events in wartime history. President Truman said fewer lives were lost in the bombings than would have been if the United States had taken part in a ground invasion. However, the decision to use atomic weapons is still debated. Do you think this was the right approach to take? Or do you think there was another way to end the war with less death and destruction? Why?

Another View

This book talks about the wartime role of Japanese emperor Hirohito and how he influenced Japan's surrender. As you know, every source is different. Ask a librarian or another adult to help you find another source about this leader. Write a short essay comparing and contrasting the new source's point of view with that of this book's author. What is the point of view of each author? How are they similar and why? How are they different and why?

Tell the Tale

Chapter One of this book discusses the celebrations that took place when Japan surrendered. Imagine you were in the crowd that day. Write 200 words about how you might have felt when you saw Truman's message in flashing lights on the Times Tower. How would you celebrate?

Surprise Me

Chapter Three discusses Japan's surrender. After reading this book, what two or three facts about the situation did you find most surprising? Write a few sentences about each fact. Why did you find each fact surprising?

GLOSSARY

anti-Semitism
discrimination against Jewish people

communist
a person who supports communism, which is a system that values common ownership over private property

economy
a nation's industry, trade, and finance

genocide
the large-scale destruction of a particular group of people

liberate
to free from enemy control

nationalist
relating to the belief that one nation is better than others and other nations should be more like it or should not exist

occupy
to take over and control another territory

refugee
a person who has fled a country for his or her safety

theater
an area where battles happen

unconditionally
with no limits or restrictions

ONLINE RESOURCES

To learn more about the victory and legacy of World War II, visit our free resource websites below.

Visit **abdocorelibrary.com** or scan this QR code for free Common Core resources for teachers and students, including vetted activities, multimedia, and booklinks, for deeper subject comprehension.

Visit **abdobooklinks.com** or scan this QR code for free additional online weblinks for further learning. These links are routinely monitored and updated to provide the most current information available.

LEARN MORE

Adams, Simon. *World War II*. DK, 2021.

Huddleston, Emma. *How the Bomb Changed Everything*. Abdo, 2022.

Lim, Angela. *World War II in the Pacific*. Abdo, 2025.

INDEX

About the Author

Heather C. Hudak has written hundreds of children's books. Heather's grandmother served in the Women's Armed Forces in London during World War II. Her grandmother's first husband was a Canadian soldier killed in action on Juno Beach on D-Day. In 2022 Heather visited his memorial in Normandy.